The Cyber Love Connection

Other books by
Stephanie Fletcher

Blinded By Love

THE CYBER LOVE CONNECTION

S. M. Fletcher

authorHOUSE®

AuthorHouse™
1663 Liberty Drive
Bloomington, IN 47403
www.authorhouse.com
Phone: 1-800-839-8640

Published by AuthorHouse   12/29/2012

ISBN: 978-1-4634-1661-4 (sc)
ISBN: 978-1-4634-1660-7 (e)

Library of Congress Control Number: 2011909248

Through my saddness, my lonelness
I began an unimaginable adventure
With memories of you I've made it
Through and learned that friendship,
And love come into our lives in all forms.

In memory of
Angela Barnes

THE GUITAR MAN

I feel like a school girl with her first crush,
I can't wait to talk to you,
Hoping one day to feel your touch.

Your words are my music,
Each word a special note,
For you are the guitar man,
And are ever so remote.

When you speak to me my heart skips a beat,
Oh my guitar man,
How I long for us to meet.

INTERNET AFFECTION

These are the days of internet affection.
The world is full of many seeking a cyber love connection.
Your anonymity to be who you please,
Puts those seeking love more at ease.

Romance sparks with a few simply words,
Leaving excitement wonder around each turn,
Preferences are stated on each profile,
But chatting it up is fun for awhile.

Internet affection the cyber love connection,
Is taking finding a mate,
In a whole different direction.

SECRET LOVER

Secret lover, that's what you are,
She found you on the internet highway of love.
Your words, so sweet,
They set her heart a flame.
How eager she is to hear from you again and again.

Secret lover that's what you are.
Ever so close, ever so far.
She dreams of meeting you and of what possibly could be,
Hoping these words you share,
Could create more between you and she.

SILENT MOMENTS

How I wait to hear from you,
These hours are so long,
Time moves here ever so slow.

We really don't know each other,
We're just words on a screen,
But when I hear from you,
My heart begins to sing.

Talking to you gives me something,
To look forward to.
My days and nights fly past,
But theses long silent moments here,
I sit feeling so sad.

YOUR VOICE

Our first phone call for me . . . was our first kiss,
The gentle sound of your voice,
As it caressed my ear, closing my eyes I can feel you near.

Your words were a simple embrace,
Letting me know what you've done through out the day,
Multitasking is what you do best,
Your children are lucky to have you;
They are truly blessed.

For me . . . your voice has lulled me off to sleep,
I can feel your breath upon my neck,
I can feel your heart beat.

My Computer and Me

Here I sit my computer and me,
While we wait for a few lines from thee,
Just a few simple lines saying I'm doing just fine,
Could hold us over for sometime.

It's been days you see, for my computer and me,
We've sent you many a line,
I hope you answer us soon,
So we can plan to spend a little time.

There's no more waiting by the phone,
For that special someone to call home,
It's the excitement of seeing,
That envelope as it bounces along.

For you've much to do and this you've explained,
But you promised to answer me again and again.
I'm lonely here, and don't know what I'll do,
If my computer and I don't hear from you.

SOMETHING LIKE THIS

I'm experiencing something I haven't felt in days,
You've given my body something it's craved.
You stirred my scenes, caused my heart to pound.
You were miles away from here,
No where near my town.

I've experienced something I never did before,
Your words ignited a passion,
That has swelled inside of me.
You entered just the right words to set me free.

I've never experienced anything like this before,
I wonder if I would, if you walked through my door.

To Instant Message

To IM or not to IM . . . . that is the question.
For it brings people closer together
Faster than e-mail, at times waiting for a response,
Can make you mad as hell.
Instant messaging a friend,
Brings you much closer together,
The conversation takes on a flow.
You can say anything, be anyone,
Who truly has to know?
E-mailing you can do the same,
But getting that on the spot response is the name of the game.

To IM or not to IM . . . . that is the question.

THE CHAT LINE

He found her while on the chat line,
There he mentioned he'd been lonely for sometime.
He said he was looking for a friend,
Someone to do things with and fall in love once again.

He found her there chatting away,
His words touched her,
She knew not what to say.
His sadness touched her heart.

You don't know me, I don't know you,
We could get to know each other,
If you would like to.

Her words made him smile,
She came across so kind.
Yes I'd like that, said he,
To have a chance to win you over and make you mine.

LOOKING OUT THE WINDOW

Looking out the window deeply how I sigh,
I can't help but miss you,
Wishing you were by my side.
I know that you're working,
But endlessly I try,
Not hunger for you,
These feelings I can't deny.
I check to see if you e-mailed,
Then silently I'd cry,
To see no message for me,
It hurts to know I'm not on your mind.

HOW CAN I MISS YOU

How can I miss someone I don't know?
The conversations shared has made me laugh,
Often after I wasn't so sad.

How can I miss someone I don't know?
Who's voice is his hands,
Caressing me with typed words,
Upon each glance.

How do we know how far this will go?
When it's only just begun?
For a few days you've stirred a passion,
I've never known before.

These days I long for those words more and more,
Craving for the promise they instill,
And the way you make me feel.

How can I miss someone I don't know?
How can I miss you more than you'll ever know?

I Looked at Her and Wondered

I looked at her and wondered . . .
Why I resented her so.
Was it because you loved her,
More than you could know?

I looked back on it to realize why,
You never truly saw me,
With those wide blue eyes,
And that you would never be mine.

Looking back on yesterday I have no regrets,
For my longing for you has opened in me,
Feelings I thought I had long forget.

I'm alive, I can feel once again,
The passion the pleasure, even the pain that love brings.

I looked at her and wondered . . .
Why did I resent her so?
It was because you loved her more than I did know.

It Began With a Flirt

It all began with a flirt . . .
A simple, I would like to talk to you,
Was all it took, before I knew it,
I was hooked.
The language was so new to me.
You laughed at how innocent I could be.

It all began with a flirt . . .
Your words touched me so,
I couldn't believe someone so far,
Could feel so near,
The words you spoke made me blush,
Making me long for you oh so much.

It began with a flirt . . .
Send me a photo, who could it hurt,
Tell me your hearts desire, and I'll tell you mine,
I promise not to play with your emotions,
I promise to never make you cry.

It all started with a flirt . . .
In the end, I did get hurt.

THE GIRL IN THE MIRROR

It has been many years since I've seen the girl in the mirror,
In years past, she was younger,
Seven or eight I can't remember the date.
My vision became a haze,
I was unable to see,
Scared and a little crazed,
The girl had gone from view,
There was nothing I could do.

Wearing thick glasses wasn't cool,
Called names, being made fun of,
Often left me feeling alone and blue.
Not pretty like my sis, I then made a wish,
For my eyes to be able to see,
Glasses upon my face, oh I how I felt so out of place.

Now here I' am, all grown up,
Face still covered in glass,
Afraid to fall in love, for fear of the past,
To change my optical wear, was all I could do,
Just to be accepted by you.
I looked in the mirror, just to see her starring back at me,
The way she use to do,

Bought a tear to my eye, just to see that I was pretty too,
It had been years since I've seen the girl in the mirror,
And wondered where she'd gone,
Just to see it was me and I was here all along.

I think I'm in Love

I think I'm in love; his words have reached my inner being.
I think I'm in love; his face I have not yet seen.
I want him close so I can see,
If he's really the man for me.
I think I'm in love; when his words don't appear upon the screen,
I get worried, angry, down right mean.
I believe I'm in love; with a stranger I met,
Here on the internet.

LONELINESS SURROUNDS ME

Loneliness surrounds me your words are what I crave,
I haven't spoken to you,
It's been six or seven days.
My heart is slowly breaking in oh so many ways,
As loneliness surrounds me,
I sit here in this place.

Emotions riding high from words from this strange guy,
Longing to be by his side,
Oh so endlessly I cry.
Shutting down the system as I pray for another day,
To see your words upon the screen,
Pushing loneliness away.

DAYS HAVE GONE BY

Days have gone by . . . .
Still I dream of you . . . .
Remembering all the things you said you could do to me,
To sooth my body and set it free.

Days have gone by . . .
Still no word from you . . .
I wonder if everything is fine,
Hoping you're not hurt or feeling blue.

How I miss our instant messaging,
The closeness that we've forged,
The passion you bought alive in me,
The way I felt when I thought you'd soon be at my door.

Days have gone by . . .
Still I dream of you . . .
So much time lost, not hearing the words I long to.

Days have gone by . . .
Still I dream of you . . .
Longing to glance upon your face,
Is all I want to do.

WHY DID HE COME THIS WAY

Why did he come this way?
Knowing he'd never be able to escape,
Wanting so to be free,
That's when he found me.

Both longing for our freedom to do as we please,
He's held by a past,
Which he seems not to be able to break free.

Why did he come this way?
I feel his pain, his despair,
Of being someplace where,
Love is no longer there.

Why did he come this way?
To find love, to find me,
Waiting with open arms to wipe away his tears,
To set his heart free.

THE PHOTO

It was his words which touched her heart,
The tenderness, the passion,
Displayed from the start,
There was no photo to catch her eye,
To hide behind a smile,
Or deceive or lie.
Desire rose between them by words alone,
A heart felt romance,
That took the world by storm.
There was no photo to catch his eye,
He wanted to see the face,
That love now hid behind.
Time went by as they chatted on,
Then he began to sing the picture song,
She sent a few shots,
This is what she got.
No messages were received,
She didn't know whether or not he was pleased,
Now she sat and wondered,
Where could he be?
There've been no e-mails,
Since that day,
It broke her heart that he
Acted this way,
Sad . . . She thought her words had touched his heart,
As his touched hers from the start.

S. M. Fletcher

My Heart

Angry and hurt;
Who would've known these feelings would come from a flirt.
His face she does not know,
How she wondered . . . could a romance could grow?
The distance between them,
So vast it seems.
He requested a picture

With a simple description,
Using his words to do a little manipulation,
Computer tag and phone hide and seek,
Were not the games for she;
Only wanted to get to know you can't you see?

To Long island . . . she lost her head.
Never realizing, being stood up could hurt so bad.
She has feelings, just like you.
She was looking for love and someone to get close to.

TODAY IS THE DAY

Today is the day I've been set free,
I could do what I want,
Go where ever I please.
This is the day I wanted to spend with you,
To walk hand and hand in the park,
To see a movie or two.

Today is the day I've been set free.
There aren't many days like this for me.
You never responded in time,
As I sit here waiting to make you mine.

The rains have come and gone,
The sky is gray,
Mother nature seemed to know things,
Would turn out this way,
But for today . . . it is the day I've been set free.
Now I lay here writing,
Of the things that should've been.

POURING RAINS

Pouring rains, deep gray skies,
Bought a tear to her eye,
Starring out onto the damp world,
She wondered why she got up at all.
Checking e-mails for a word or too,
Left her broken hearted and blue.
Pouring rains, deep gray skies,
Made her wonder, If she ever crossed your mind?
Often you said you thought of her,
On lonely days like this,
She wasn't sure.
Pouring rains, deep gray skies,
Left a longing deep inside.

ENVY

Her heart was overjoyed with anticipation of the day,
For her new love would be coming her way.
Communication via the net,
Was the way the couple met.

For me, my heart doesn't sing,
There's no joy for me,
For you've gone far away you see,
You promised to write often as you can,
I search the net, but you weren't there.

Envy has taken hold of me,
For how I long to be with thee.
I tell her not to speak of the things she'll endure,
Because I can't take it anymore,

Envy has its hold on me,
I long for you so desperately.
She says his words are like fire,
And she's drawn to his flame,

I remember our conversations and feeling just the same.
But how envy has its hold on me,
I hate this longing feeling,
How I want for you to release me.

A FRIENDS JOY

I'm glad she's found someone who loves her,
Someone who looks beyond her imperfections
As though they weren't there,
Happiness she deserves as many of us do,
Out of many who've crossed her path,
You were the nicest,
She's found at last.
I'm glad she smiles now for there were many tears,
For there's one who caused her to do that for years.
We giggle like girls at the sight of her e-mails,
And how sweet your words have been from the start,
But while she shares her joy,
I can't help think about my special boy,

THIS THING I FEEL

This thing I feel . . . has consumed me,
I have no idea what it could be.
It came upon me when you had gone,
Your words were missing,
I was left all alone.

What was to be a few weeks assignment,
Has now become mandatory confinement,
As I sit by the computer,
Waiting for those words I long for.

This thing I feel . . . which has consumed me,
Has left me as miserable as can be.
How can I explain what I feel?
If I don't know what it is?

I set out to find a friend,
Someone to pal around with every now and then,
Then there came you, with words of fire,
Stirring me as no one could ever do.

But now . . . this thing I feel . . .
Ooh how it consumes me,
The longing deep inside I can no longer deny,
The feelings I have for thee.

PHAT GIRLS NEED LOVE

She wondered if you'd never seen her picture would you care.
She wondered if a romance would grow, would you be there.
Warned she wasn't a size eight,
She sent photos, and then wished she'd hesitate.
Days went by and no word from you,
Often she wondered where you went off to.
Finally she got the hint,
How unkind the way things went.
How cruel of you to break her heart,
She thought you were different from the start.
You were just like all the rest,
Wanting a fashion plate to lie upon your chest.
Oh what a silly fool,
Don't you know phat girls need love to?
Her heart was yours to have and hold,
The loss of her love you'll never know.

I CRIED ENOUGH

I think I cried enough today,
I pray my heart can take another day,
To overcome such despair,
While waiting to have you near,
I think I've cried enough today,
As I pray to God to send love my way,
I think I've cried enough today.

I Go On

What a difference a day makes,
To wake though my heart is heavy . . . I go on.
You are constantly on my mind,
Probably will be for sometime . . . But I go on.
Checking different sites,
My heart tells me it isn't right,
I do what I must . . . I go on.
Could this be love I feel or cyber lust?
For me right now, checking profiles is a must,
To combat my feelings for you so . . . I go on.
Hoping for the day, when you IM my way,
To see if the spark is still alive,
But for now . . . I go on.

A Fear of Love

Her heart belongs to another who has a fear of love,
Pushing her away, he doesn't realize what he does.
Tears fill her eyes,
For the love she can't deny,
He sees it, yet still pushes it aside.
Her pain undeniable,
How she long for its release,
Dinner with friends a weekend trip out east.
For her heart belongs to another,
Who has a fear of love,
He keeps pushing her away never realizing what he does.

A TIME OF TRAGEDY

This has been a week of tragedy,
From the loss of a home, to the death of an unborn baby,
In these times fate has chose to be so unkind,
To the point of driving many out of they're minds.

This has been a time of tragedy,
There are two young men who may lose a gift that is most
cherished,
Simply by taking it from another,
In these times the world has changed,
Leaving in its midst nothing but suffering and pain.

This is a time of tragedy,
As we remember the day two were loss,
And the thousands that filled their hallowed halls,
Of the many who forge on,
Maintaining a strong and steady course.

This is the time to have faith,
To believe in the one who will help us make it through these trying
days.

TRAVELING THE GLOBE

There in the chat room she found a different world,
Traveling across the globe, she was never alone.
She loved in Paris and in Rome, in Egypt and Morocco,
Africa left her with a feeling of despair,
While she danced in India without a care.
She traveled to the Netherlands, Texas, London and back,
Never a dull moment did she lack.
Hawaii was the best, the kindest gentlest state,
Above all the rest.
There in the chat room,
She can be who she pleased,
To pretend to fall in love or to be just a tease.
Traveling across the globe,
She goes where she wants and is never alone.

UNTRUE WERE YOUR WORDS

You said I was never forgotten . . .
Oh how untrue were your words,
You said you wouldn't play with my emotions . . .
Oh how untrue were your words.

Many days I've sat here waiting to hear from thee,
You said you wanted to be free . . .
How you longed to be with me,
Oh how untrue were you words.

Months have gone by,
Without one single line from the one I wanted by my side,
There would be days I did sit and cry,
Wondering why my love you pushed aside.
You said I was never forgotten . . .
Oh how untrue were your words.

I SAW YOU ON THE IM

Today I saw you on the IM,
I couldn't wait to hear from you once again.
You never acknowledged me,
I couldn't believe you would do this to me.
Today I saw you on the IM,
I wrote to you as I've done back then,
You sent me no reply,
You said you'd never hurt me,
On this I could rely.
But you slammed the door in my face,
Oh then how I cried.
All I wanted was to see where we stood,
If what I thought we had was still good.
I saw you on the IM,
A stranger in my midst,
How could things change so fast?
Why did it end like this?
Today I saw you on the IM,
I waited to hear from you as I did then,
You never acknowledged me,
Now we've come to an end.

MIND, HANDS AND HEART

She loved him from a far with her,
Mind, hands and heart,
What began as a chat,
Suddenly became more than that.
Often he spoke of how things would be,
He dreamed of the day he'd be free,
Of how he longed to love again,
To be with someone who was more than a lover,
But his friend,
He loved her from a far with his,
Mind, hands and heart,
Who would've known a love like that?
Simply began with a chat.

A HUSBAND

A husband . . . that's what he was,
Married for years to the one he loved,
Her desires had turned cold,
Blaming her age she claimed to be too old,
For sharing the passion,
That once was there.
For many a night the husband sat in despair,
A husband . . . that's what he was,
Sitting at the computer just to get a buzz,
Looking to find a friend,
Someone to talk with every now and then,
There he found her,
Ready to please willing to put his body at ease,
With a few simple words,
That's all it took,
Then the husband new he was hooked.

A New Day

He has made her smile again,
Easing away the pain,
She thinks of you now and then,
Realizing how things have changed.
He's made her smile again,
With the things he say and do,
Keeping her busy so she won't have to think of you,
You told her how glad you were,
To have her in your life,
That you gladly marry her,
If you didn't have a wife,
He's made her smile again,
Easing away her pain,
Making her glad again to see a new day.

It's Hard to Imagine

It's hard to imagine just how times have changed,
It seems like forever ago when you were all I wanted,
All I longed for.
Now here I sit,
Head in hands longing to be free,
Searching for the words to say,
Trying to make it easy to leave,
It's hard to imagine,
Falling out of love,
With one who was there from the start.
It was you who wiped away my tears, who turned my frown into a smile.
Time has passed,
I've changed so,
It's hard to imagine my life without you,
Things being as they are, there's nothing else I can do.

S. M. Fletcher

WHAT ARE YOU SEEKING?

Who are you seeking?
Who could it be?
Or is it someone who can satisfy thee?
What are you seeking?
Do you know?
Someone to be with while you're on the go?
The internet is your link,
To travel the world,
Making friends of all races, while going to many places.
What is it you're seeking?
Do you even know?
Could it be the freedom you lost so long ago?

TIME WITH MY MOTHER

This has been the time I've spent with my mother,
It's been the best for us by far.
It does my heart good to see her take a break,
Leaving behind the daily grind,
Taking time for a little piece of mind.
This is my time with my mother,
A chance to show her just how much I love her,
Hoping to leave a memory of this time we've shared,
Letting her know I'll always be there.
For those in her life left behind,
I wish they understand how I need this time,
For this is the time I'm spending with my mother,
Just to show her how much I love her.

S. M. Fletcher

DRIFTING AWAY

Drifting far away at sea,
I sit here longing for thee,
How I ache to IM you,
It is all I want to do.
Drifting far away at sea,
Mother sees a change in me,
She wonders what has caused the change,
Slowly I whisper out your name,
Drifting far away at sea,
In our cabin she watches T.V.
As I look across the sea,
Wondering if you miss me,
Drifting far away at sea,
I can't wait to get home where I should be,
Just to be close to you,
Is all I long to do.

FRIENDS AND LOVERS

The fall sky, so crisp and blue,
Makes me wonder what you're up too.
If your evening sky shines bright,
Do the stars there dance with delight?
Here in the sun I dream of us having fun,
Strolling hand and hand,
Tossing leaves about, without a care.
In my nights I long for you,
Wondering during your days where you go to.
If you see me on your streets,
As you go about your day,
Do you long for me in the worst way?
My nights are your days,
How I wish we'd find a way,
To make out time as one,
But until that day, our computers are the way,
We have a little fun.
To become friends as well as lovers,
As we discover one another.

A MOMENT TO ONE SELF

Privacy that moment to one self,
To do what you please,
Has become a lost commodity for me.
We all need time alone,
To chat on the computer or telephone,
Being with loved ones is just fine,
Sharing a movie, going out to dine.
For me, privacy that moment to one self,
Is something most cherished in it self.

The Cyber Love Connection

By S.M. Fletcher

While seeking to fulill loneliness the internet has become
Away to meet people, to be who you want to be
To be who you are without being judged by what you
Look like or what you may or may not have.

A simple hello can open up so much and before you know it . . .
You are hooked.
Just like in the real world, you fall in and out of love.
The joy and the pain is no different.

About the author

A resident of Long Island NY Stephanie lives in the town of Coram
With her family. She employed by Department of Treasury. She enjoys
Traveling and meeting new people.